First World War
and Army of Occupation
War Diary
France, Belgium and Germany

57 DIVISION
Divisional Troops
173 Machine Gun Company
1 May 1917 - 1 March 1918

WO95/2974/5

The Naval & Military Press Ltd
www.nmarchive.com
Published in association with The National Archives

Published by

The Naval & Military Press Ltd

Unit 10 Ridgewood Industrial Park,

Uckfield, East Sussex,

TN22 5QE England

Tel: +44 (0) 1825 749494

www.naval-military-press.com

www.nmarchive.com

This diary has been reprinted in facsimile from the original. Any imperfections are inevitably reproduced and the quality may fall short of modern type and cartographic standards.

© Crown Copyright
Images reproduced by permission of The National Archives, London, England, 2015.

Contents

Document type	Place/Title	Date From	Date To
Heading	WO95/2974-5		
Heading	173rd Machine Gun Coy. May 1917-1918 Feb		
War Diary	Armentieres Defence	01/05/1917	30/06/1917
Heading	D A G 3rd Echelon	12/11/1917	12/11/1917
War Diary	Armentieres Defences	01/07/1917	30/09/1917
War Diary	La Tirmand	01/10/1917	31/10/1917
War Diary	Langemarck	01/11/1917	07/11/1917
War Diary	Boesinghe	08/11/1917	09/11/1917
War Diary	Clerques	10/11/1917	07/12/1917
War Diary	Herzeele	07/12/1917	16/12/1917
War Diary	Sutton Camp	17/12/1917	24/12/1917
War Diary	Luneville Farm	26/12/1917	26/12/1917
War Diary	Dublin Camp	28/12/1917	04/01/1918
War Diary	Armentieres Defences	05/01/1918	11/01/1918
Miscellaneous	173 Machine Gun Company. Operation Order No. 1	04/01/1918	04/01/1918
Miscellaneous	173 Machine Gun Company. Operation Order No. 2	10/01/1918	10/01/1918
Miscellaneous	173 Machine Gun Company. Operation Order No. 3	21/01/1918	21/01/1918
War Diary	Armentieres Defences	01/02/1918	14/02/1918
War Diary	Armentiers	15/02/1918	15/02/1918
War Diary	Chappelle Duvelle (Estaires)	15/02/1918	28/02/1918
Miscellaneous	173rd M.G. Coy. Operation Order No. 4	12/02/1918	12/02/1918
Miscellaneous	57 Div.		
War Diary	Map Sheet 36A N.E.		
War Diary	Chapelle Duvelle	16/02/1918	15/03/1918
War Diary	Boisgrenier Fleurbaix Padinghem Aubers	21/03/1918	21/03/1918
War Diary	Croix Du Bac	31/03/1918	31/03/1918
War Diary	Chappelle Duvelle	01/03/1918	01/03/1918

2967/2974 ⑤ m06m

2967/2974 ⑤ m06m

57TH DIVISION

173RD MACHINE GUN COY.

MAY 1917 ~~MAY 1919~~

1918 FEB

WAR DIARY

OF 173 M.G. Coy

Army Form C. 2118.

INTELLIGENCE SUMMARY

FOR MAY 1917

PAGE 1

Instructions regarding War Diaries and Intelligence Summaries are contained in F.S. Regs., Part II. and the Staff Manual respectively. Title Pages will be prepared in manuscript.

Place	Date	Hour	Summary of Events and Information	Remarks and references to Appendices
ARMENTIERES DEFENCES	1/5/17		Condition normal on our front. Visibility good. N° 58272 PTE CARTER. E to hospital sick. Casualties Officer. W.U. O.R. N.U.	
"	2/5/17	9.30 AM	ARMENTIERES was shelled about 9.30AM, several being shell. (S.97) fell near our Company Line (Sh.36 N.W.2 (9C 30.30) Casualties W.U. N° 58814 PTE GORDON.N & N° 58813 PTE PARKINSON to hospital sick. N° PTE ROBERTSON joined the Coy from the BASE & was on strength of Coy. Visibility was good & with the exception of shelling mentioned condition normal.	
"	3/5/17		There is nothing to report N° 53505 P(CPL) MOORE, JH, N° 54659 PTE JONES.S.A. to Marshall sick. C. SECTION under 2nd LT BUSHELL. Relieved A. SECTION LT FISHER at NORTH HOUPLINES & D. SECTION 2nd LT BROCK was relieved by B. SECTION 2nd LT HARRISON at SOUTH HOUPLINES. Casualties Officers W.U. O.R. nil.	
"	4/5/17		A quiet day. Visibility was poor. Early morning heavy but late was good. N° 58960 P(CPL) LAKE T.W to FIELD AMBCE sick. The Mairie at NORTH HOUPLINES (Sh.W.36 N.W.2, C.21.B. T.S. 20) was set on fire by a bomb from an aeroplane. A SECTION under 2nd LT. FISHER who was billeted in the same street did their best to put it out but designs wanting. S.A.A. bombs etc & covers munitions at were by R.E. dumps were all to doubtful & the work was guttered. No truth, however remain nearlier to find trouble cover from M.G. Fire. Casualties Off. W.U. O.R. N.U.	
"	5/5/17		Visibility is about half of the day quiet. During the night of 5/6 these was heavy shelling on our B/EPINETTE Sector & Shell fell in ARMENTIERES Sh36 S.U 35 N.W. 22 S.E 30 S.E. about 2.15 AM	

WAR DIARY / INTELLIGENCE SUMMARY

OF 173 M.G. Coy
MAY 1917
PAGE II

Army Form C. 2118.

Place	Date	Hour	Summary of Events and Information	Remarks and references to Appendices
ARMENTIRES	6/5/17	3.30 AM	The Town was shelled about 3.30 A.M. At 4 A.M. all was quiet again & the rest of the day was normal.	
DEFENCES	7/5/17		The day was quiet. At 7.15 P.M. we heard a heavy bombardment in the EPINETTE SECTOR. We were informed by our Section in HOUPLINES NORTH that their Division to & movement their position the were absorbed by the Section at SOUTH HOUPLINES. The remaining two Sections at H.Q. stood to receive orders about 7.45 P.M. We had the gun claims bow & furnite on hut or adjusted. By the orders of the O.C. Coy, 2 guns of the Section in reserve moved to BRIGADE H.Q from there to our position B.H.Q might consider necessary. (These were 2 of C. Sect Guns.) The remaining 2 guns of C. SECTION under 2"LT BRIANT moved to V.G.P. at Shaft 36NW I.D.9030 & I.14.00.00 & the other mid-section NISBETT took up position at 36NW I.2.C.30.70 & I.2.C.16.60 of D. were in position at 36NWC 21.c30.30 & 21.c.04.28. About 9.30 P.M. we heard that the guns claims were a brush-out of moments were removed but-left at the alert in position. A heavy bombardment was kept up all the time & the even reached our trenches first on the HOUPLINES SECTOR about 8 P.M. on trenches 15,16,17 & 10.30.40 to G.M.Q. 00.20. This attack was driven off the HOUPLINES SECTOR & punched down at 9.40 P.M. Several lights this turning on to trenches 5,6,7 - T.3. C.25.20 - I.5.a.40.80 where is our main head obtained a position at 9.10 P.M. Germans. Then our guns put down a heavy barrage on the spot. After the enemy had been driven out	

WAR DIARY
193 M.G. Coy
INTELLIGENCE SUMMARY MAY 1917 PAGE III

Army Form C. 2118.

Place	Date	Hour	Summary of Events and Information	Remarks and references to Appendices
ARMENTIERES	7/5/17	(contd)	Our Section were about to proceed down & return to billets when they were ordered to remain in their position as the Enemy Artillery were to open a shoot along the whole army front. This was carried out, the enemy being provoked to shell the Town at intervals of half an hour. The shoot down stream trawl about 4.15 a.m. + the Section returned to billets. Our Casualties Officers NIL O.R. NIL	
DEFENCES	8/5/17		The day has been quiet & there is nothing to report	
"	9/5/17		2nd Lieut FISHER & a SECTION who are at NORTH HOUPLINES report that their neighbourhood 36NW2 C21B50 have shelled with shells of large calibre this morning, the enemy also shelled ARMENTIERES from 12 noon — 8 P.M. Casualties Officers NIL O.R. NIL	
"	10/5/17		Conditions have normal, there is nothing to report	
"	11/5/17		nothing to report	
"	12/5/17		do.	
"	13/5/17		LIEUT WELLS Casualties LIEUT. A.H. WELLS (field to hospital) O.R. nil	
"	14/5/17		nothing to report.	
"	15/5/17		Nothing to report	

WAR DIARY of 173 M.G. Coy
INTELLIGENCE SUMMARY
For MAY 1917
Page IV

Army Form C. 2118.

Place	Date	Hour	Summary of Events and Information	Remarks and references to Appendices
ARMENTIÈRES DEFENCES.	16/5/17		The day was very quiet and there seemed to be a marked decrease in enemy artillery fire.	1110
"	17/5/17		Another quiet day. Visibility poor. A Section under 2nd Lt FISHER relieved C Section. 2nd Lt BUSHELL 4 D Section 2nd Lt BROCK was relieved by B Section under 2nd Lt HARRISON. At 8.15 PM B Section at N HOUPLINES S60rd 16 and manned their positions during a short bombardment by the enemy on the left of our Divisional Front. 2nd Lt HARRISON ordered his section to stand down at 9 p.m. after normal conditions had been resumed. Casualties Nil.	1110
"	18/5/17		Enemy artillery on our front very inactive. Nothing to report.	1113
"	19/5/17		A quiet day. Harry received information that the enemy had brought pontoons to the River Lys at C 11 a central and C 11 b central (Ref map Armentières 36 N.W.2 1/20000) Indirect fire was carried out by B Section at Houplines with from the following positions C 21.b 8010, C 21.b 8505, C 21.b 9005 between 10 pm and midnight. Lieut Machen proceeded to Camera on Machine Gun Course.	1113
"	20/5/17		Nothing to report except increased M.G. fire by the enemy in the Houplines + Epinette sections during the early part of the night	1110
"	21/5/17		Generally a quiet day. Enemy made use of several star shells bursting into different colour which remained a long time in the air. Indirect fire from C 21.b 5340 traversing between C 10 b 9030 and C 11 a 4510 (Ref map 36 N.W. 1/20000) A fire in enemy line opened at 10 p.m. on a TB of 30° from C 21.b 5340	1110
"	22/5/17		Wet day, visibility bad. Enemy retired to the making much greater use of machine gun against our	1113

Army Form C. 2118.

WAR DIARY OF 173 M.G. Coy
or INTELLIGENCE SUMMARY.
For MAY 1917
Page V

(Erase heading not required.)

Place	Date	Hour	Summary of Events and Information	Remarks and references to Appendices
ARMENTIERES DEFENCES	24/5/17 (cont'd)		Aeroplane Indirect fire was carried out by us from C21.b.55.40 against targets C.5.c.70.10 and C.11.c.35.85. (Ref. Map 36 NW.1/20000) 2nd Lt. MILLWARD B joined the Company and was posted to B Section	MR
"	25/5/17		A fine day. Aerial activity much increased. Enemy showed little making more use of Trenches from aspect: our aircraft. The following targets were engaged by us indirect fire. C.5.c.70.05 to C.11.b.31.85. C.11.c.71.75. C.11.c.90.35. & C.11.d.35.00. (Ref. Map 36 NW.1/20000)	MR
"	26/5/17	"	The day passed quietly. C. Section under 2nd Lt. BRANT relieved B Section 2nd Lt. HARRISON. D Section under 2nd Lt. BECK relieved A Section 2nd Lt. FISHER.	MR
"	26/5/17	"	Nothing to report. Indirect fire on C.11.c.70.75 & C.11.b.33.90 and C.11.c.33.55 (Ref. Map 36 NW 1/20000)	MR
"	27/5/17	"	Situation normal, aerial activity increased. Indirect fire on C.22.c.05.75 (Ref. Map 36 NW 2 1/20000).	MR
"	28/5/17	"	A quiet day. Indirect fire on C.11.c.85.91 from C.21.a.80.20. 2/Lt Lebrun thought not scale fire killed at the Trestle artillery more active, about 200 shells falling in vicinity of C.21.b.30.50. without doing any	MR
"	29/5/17		material damage. Nothing to report	MR
"	30/5/17		Situation quiet. Enemy strafe in front of C.11.c.87.41 from C.21.b.90.07. also from C.22.c.05.75 at front below C.11.c.0000 & C.18.c.80.20. 2/Lt Lebrun thought not scale fire. killed at the Trestle with indirect Hopkins and Ide place.	MR
"	31/5/17		A quiet day. Indirect inspection of men pulled in relation 1 man above being cancelled. Strength of Company on 31/5/17. 12 off. 173 o.r. Reinforcements received during month 1 off. 50 o.r.	MR

WAR DIARY of 173 Machine Gun Company. Army Form C. 2118.

JUNE 1917 Vol Page I

INTELLIGENCE SUMMARY.

Place	Date	Hour	Summary of Events and Information	Remarks and references to Appendices
Armentières Defences.	1917 1 June	12 noon	Present Strength of Company 12 noon 1/6/17. 11 officers 168 O.R. 54 animals. A quiet day with following 2 Report. Between 10 p.m. & 12 p.m. C11a 8005 from C21b 6540 and C18c 0000 to C18c 8020 from C27c 0575 (Map Ref Sc. 36 NW2 & NE1 10000. S. Straight increased by S.O.R. transferred to us from No 172 M.G. Coy.	A/3.
"	2 June		Artillery activity increasing on the left of divisional front. be carried out. Individual fire from C22C 0575 on C18C 0000 to	A/3.
"	3 June		C18C 8020 and from C21b 6540 on C11c 8005. Our Artillery very active from ARMENTIÈRES North to YPRES during the night and most of the day. 6000 rounds expended by us on indirect fire during the night.	A/3.
"	4 June		Enemy shelled back area during the day and night. Considerable artillery activity and counter battery fire on the left of our divisional front. 2000 rounds expended by us in indirect fire during the night.	A/3.
"	5 June		Enemy Artillery again very active shelling back area. C11c 3588 fired upon from C21b 6540 during the night.	A/3.
"	6 June		Armentières town shelled during the day. Our 9 p.m. sections shoot to D Section under 2nd Lt BROCK proceeding to CASTLE BELLINGHAM (C 20 & 73) A Section under 2nd Lt BROCK FISHER proceeded to WEST YORKS LOCALITY, C Section standing by in N. HOUPLINES, & B Section remaining in reserve in ARMENTIÈRES — the above was carried out in anticipation of enemy operations consequent upon the attack by our troops at MESSINES and WYTSCHAETE which commenced at 3.10 a.m. on the 7th inst. 8000 rounds expended on indirect fire from N. HOUPLINES on C11c 3588, C11d 5005 and C21c 9044.	M/3.
"	7th		Enemy shelled back area again during the day, N HOUPLINES town shelled during the afternoon C 21 d central and the road between C21d 72 and C27 c 28 received most attention. 2nd Lt HARRISON and 2.O.R. proceeded to FOSSE on Anti-Aircraft Course.	A/3.

WAR DIARY of No 173 MACHINE GUN COMPANY

INTELLIGENCE SUMMARY. JUNE 1917.

Army Form C. 2118.

Page 2.

(Erase heading not required.)

Place	Date	Hour	Summary of Events and Information	Remarks and references to Appendices
Armentieres Defences	1917 June 8		During the afternoon & evening enemy shelled back areas to the North of ARMENTIERES. Orders have been received from Divison that Reserve (1/3 Battalion (2) of 1/2 Bde Brigade would if felt in holding to support 171st Bde. Arrangements were made for this distribution. Our areas defended by the Company & such defensive mg's as necessary. At night, enemy shelled the work front of the Town and areas beyond - 30 o.r. were wounded and 4 o.r. killed. Lt NEEDHAM returned to unit from Arty. Course at CAMIERS	14D. 14B
"	June 9		Enemy shelled N. HOUPLINES and ARMENTIERES during the day - also considerable shelling of back areas chiefly in new trench in C23d at C23a 77 in Enemy again shelled back areas ARMENTIERES & HOUPLINES being shelled persistently. A fire broke out in Armentieres	14B
"	" 10.		ARMENTIERES at 10.30 pm caused by battle shelling. No further 5 hours. During operations on the left of Divisional front two rods in N HOUPLINES old W.YPERS were shelled extensively. We expended 4000 rounds on indirect fire at C11C 3588 and C11C 8705. No aircraft seen - visibility bad.	14B
"	" 11		A dull day with rain in the morning. ARMENTIERES and back areas were again shelled at intervals throughout the day and night. A raid by the enemy took place at 9.30 pm on HOUPLINES Sector. We fired from C27B8x73 on C23d 1060 (front line support of enemy) in support. All quiet by 10.30 pm.	14B
"	" 12		ARMENTIERES and back areas shelled persistently during the day and night. We fired on C11C 3588 from C21B6x90 during the night. Our Transport have moved to been lines at H3 b/33525.	14B
"	" 13		A quiet day. Fewer shells falling in back areas FRELINGHEIN was carefully watched from O.P. in N. HOUPLINES to ascertain if any unusual movement were taking place there or any signs of enemy withdrawal. During the night we fired 5000 rounds on C11C 7070 and C11C 3588 and neighbourhood. Rendezvous. 8 o.r. arrived. No rolls killed, no Transport Line	14B
"	" 14		FRELINGHEIN carefully watched from O.P. in N. HOUPLINES & S. HOUPLINES, conditions appeared normal. We carried out indirect fire on C11C 3587 and C11C 9035. 6500 rounds expended. 500 rounds on Railway Church at FRELINGHEIN fire dismounted morning preparation. Her shelling of back areas. 4 Signallers attached to Coy from 171st Bde.	14B
"	" 15		Enemy shelled ARMENTIERES and N HOUPLINES. Rapid fire during the night Barrage fire on FRELINGHEIN during the day.	14D
"	" 16		A quieter day. Enemy artillery only fire live. 300 rounds expended on indirect fire on C18C7320+C18C5060.	14B

2/Lt MILLARD 1/5 Hospital cut.

WAR DIARY of No 173 Machine Gun Company

Army Form C. 2118.

INTELLIGENCE SUMMARY.

JUNE 1917.
Page 3

Place	Date	Hour	Summary of Events and Information	Remarks and references to Appendices
Armentieres Defences	1917 June 17		FRELINGHEIN line carefully watched following any signs of enemy movement or withdrawal. A quieter day with less enemy activity. Similar activity increased. Harrasing gunfire fired on C18C & C18D30 and C18C43 & C18D16 enemy activity. Shots made reported in unusual fire.	H/B
"	June 18		Weather during Hindenburg prevailed. We fired on C1PC22 & C18D56 (300 round expended) A quieter day. The 2nd M.G. Coy Artillery Barrage. Relief Officers arrived and relieved for duty. Barrage enemy OR. Lytton wounded on duty with C company in Belgium. Enemy placed barrage shelling ARMENTIERES during the day. Ammunition of 2nd M.G. Coy PSF commenced. 300 rounds expended in barrage fire on C1PC6, C1PD6, C1PD8, B30 N4430 & C 30.0 g 9 g 8. Enemy shelled on B46a w. 25 yds	H/B
"	19		at C27.009 Stretchertown during the day	H/B H/B
"	20		Wind unsettled clearer. Bodies from /ARMENTIERES shelled heavy during the day. Our letters at 5/HOUPLINES shelled at intervals	H/B
"	21		A quieter day in ARMENTIERES. Red artillery activity. CATTLE BELLINGHAM (C20 C63) shelled by 5'9's. One man killed during the day. One O.R. wounded during the afternoon. 100 yds NW of 17th. 9 by a shoot while a bird by a man tending pigeon. Our front line & the place.	H/B
"	22		The Coy fired in Y.M.W.A. to YORKS (C27 C1079) again shelled heavily at 1.30 p.m. to 2.30 am. Our O.R. L. Lapsell with shell note. The fired at C1PC2 & C1PD18 (2500 rds expended)	H/B
"	23		A quiet day. Back arms shelled at intervals during the night	H/B
"	24		We fired on C1PC22 and C 18 d 56 (3000 rounds) Nothing to report.	H/B
"	25		Back arms again shelled at intervals during the day. ARMENTIERES shelled during the night. An 10 pm. Our enemy stands minefield emplacement now suddenly. Our HOUPLINES shells to intervals rate & 2 M.G. for PSF. (intended we for kasing) in stand routine.	H/B
"	26		A quieter day ARMENTIERES shelled at night. 300 rounds in intermittent fire	H/B
"	27		2nd Lt HARRISON & 3 O.R. returned from Instructional Course. A few returns of phorgene fell in ARMENTIERES during the night. 5 Red aeroplanes flew over our front during the day. Violent thunderstorms during the night.	H/B
"	28		Zero shelling of front area during the day. We fired on C1PC82 & C1PD56 during the night. 10.30 pm. B.hly shelled ARMENTIERES continuously from 11pm to Kindnight. 4 Aeroplanes observed overhead Watcrabit	H/B
"	29		Enemy active to shell ARMENTIERES + HOUPLINES till 3 a.m. 12pm to 3 O.R. present on N HOUPLINES All back burn in bullring killed. 2 quiet days during the day. 2 aeroplanes seen active. We fired on C 21 c g 0 5 taken on 28 any/Oz	H/B
"	30		C 24 d 89 (4000 rounds. A quiet day. Lt Witter + 2nd Lt Pengelly arrived + taken on strength. 30 to ant Cummings Course. 12 O.R. 170 OR. HQ annexed.	H/B

Strength of Company on 30th June

DAAG
3rd Echelon

War Diary for 173rd Machine Gun
Company forwarded herewith

R.B.Madden. Br.
Major General
Commanding 57 Div.

D.1117

Army Form C. 2118.

WAR DIARY of 173 Machine Gun Company
INTELLIGENCE SUMMARY.
(Erase heading not required.)

JULY 1917 Page 1 Vol 3

Instructions regarding War Diaries and Intelligence Summaries are contained in F.S. Regs., Part II. and the Staff Manual respectively. Title pages will be prepared in manuscript.

Place	Date	Hour	Summary of Events and Information	Remarks and references to Appendices
ARMENTIERES DEFENCES	1 July		Strength of Company 1 July 1917 12 officers 170 o.r. 47 rounds	
"	2 "		N. HOUPLINES shelled at intervals during the day. Enemy aircraft active flying low over trenches during the morning	MTS
"	2 "		Heavy shelling in N HOUPLINES and parts of ARMENTIERES. We fired on C24 a 00 and C24 b 05 during the night. Enemy aircraft again active over trenches during the morning. (Map Ref Sheet 36 N W 2 NE1 1/10000)	MTS
"	3 "		3000 rounds expended by us on C24 a 00 & C24 b 05 during the night. Enemy artillery again very active on N HOUPLINES. Considerable counter battery fire by enemy on ARMENTIERES, also shelling at intervals during the night.	MTS
"	4 "		N. HOUPLINES shelled at intervals during the day. We fired on C24 a 00 & C24 b 30 during the night. 3000 rounds expended on midnight fire – The N HOUPLINES road & L YORKS locality shelled at intervals during the night.	MTS
"	5 "		the day. Both areas ARMENTIERES shelled during the night.	MTS
"	6 "		Increased amount of aerial activity – ARMENTIERES & HOUPLINES shelled at intervals – We fired 6000 rounds on C18 c 82, C18 d 56 & C29 b 15	MTS MTT
"	7 "		Aerial activity increased again. ARMENTIERES shelled again day & night. 3000 rounds to midnight fire. The 2nd M.G. by P.E.F. which had been attached to us for training since 16th June. Left by pre Staal own division.	MTT
"	8 "		Continuous shelling in N. HOUPLINES during the day – ARMENTIERES quiet – We fired 6000 rounds on C24 a 00 & C24 b 05 & C29 b 83 & C 30 a 45.	MT1
"	9 "		Counter battery shelling in ARMENTIERES, a large party in C252 action fire until 1 hour all day. 5000 rounds on midnight fire. 107 C M G attached to 171 Mc. Coy.	MB.

WAR DIARY

of 173 Machine Gun Company

Army Form C. 2118.

INTELLIGENCE SUMMARY.
(Erase heading not required.)

Page 2.   JULY 1917.

Place	Date	Hour	Summary of Events and Information	Remarks and references to Appendices
ARMENTIERES DEFENCES.	1917. 11 July		Considerable aerial activity. NORTH HOUPLINES again heavily shelled during the day – also considerable shelling of Back areas and ARMENTIERES. We fired 3,000 rounds. In indirect fire – 1 N.C.O. wounded by enemy m.g. fire. 'A' Section under 2nd Lt. FISHER detailed for duty with 170 M.G. Coy. still further orders.	H³.
"	12 July		N. HOUPLINES again shelled at intervals during day and night – At 11-10 p.m. 2 officers + 24 O.R. with 4 guns of No.15 M.M.G. Battery arrived + were attached to this Coy. for duty. The riffles 'A' Section. During the night indirect fire by m.m on C24a.00, C24b.85, C24c.30 and C24d.30 + C30a.44 – 6000 rounds expended.	H³.
"	13 "		ARMENTIERES and HOUPLINES regularly shelled during the day. Considerable aerial activity. We fired 4000 rounds on C23d.50 C29d.60, C24c.30 and C20c.30. Duly with N HOUPLINES and N.YPRES Roads (C26 d.25) shelled.	H³.
"	14 "		Enemy artillery active during the morning – quieter during the afternoon – trouble in ARMENTIERES searched for Battery position. Heavy shelling on HOUPLINES and Cathy-firing gun in W2 C21b.52 - no casualties.	H³.
"	15 "		A quiet day. Very little shelling of back areas during the day. 'A' Section under 2nd Lt. FISHER returned from 170 M.G. Coy when they had been attached for duty at 11-30 a.m. We fired 7,000 rounds in indirect fire against normal targets.	H³.
"	16.		Several air fights in ARMENTIERES between 10.10 & 11a.m. At 9-04 p.m 2 officers + 24 O.R. with 4 guns of No.15 M.M.G. Battery, which had been attached to us since 12th inst., returned to their unit at 2.000 yds.	H³.
"	17		Nothing to report.	E.N.
"	18		Nothing to report.	
"	19		Strength 12 officers, 176 O.R.	S.N.
"	20		ARMENTIERES heavily bombarded at night by Gas Shells.	S.N.
"	21		1 O.R. wounded (gasproving) mgn. Shells fired in the town.	D.N.
"	22		ARMENTIERES heavily shelled all day. 5 O.R. killed 10 R wounded.	S.N.
"	23		Shelling continued gas + H.E. Suffren.	

WAR DIARY
INTELLIGENCE SUMMARY
(Erase heading not required.)

of 173 Machine Gun Company.

JULY 1917 Page 3

Army Form C. 2118.

Place	Date	Hour	Summary of Events and Information	Remarks and references to Appendices
ARMENTIERES DEFENCES	July 24		Enemy artillery less active during the day. C27 c1.7 was shelled by H.E. during the morning. C26 b.c.3 was shelled by shrapnel during the afternoon. At 11.30 pm gas shells were sent to C.27.c.5.8, C.27 a.4.7, C.26 d.4.7. 12.30 a.m 25.7.17 All clear.	2.B.I.
"	25		Quiet all day in British ARMENTIERES + HOUPLINES. "TOGO" at night. Retaliation. Shelling well to the front of emplacements. Eight guns fired 25000 rounds, nil casualties	2.B.2.
"	26		Hostile artillery very quiet in HOUPLINES. A few shrapnel sent over C.26 b & d during the afternoon. Carried out Traversing fire at night from C.23 d.50 to C.29 d.60. Ammn. exp: 2000 rounds. Heavy local shelling in ARMENTIERES at night from about 9 pm till midnight.	
"	27.		"Nothing to Report"	
"	28.		Hostile artillery has been very active in the locality during morning & afternoon of 28.7.17. This locality (NOUVEL HOUPLINES) was shelled 8.30 a.m. to 9.20 a.m. & 10.15 am to 2.30 pm. These were 4.2" were sent at an average of 8 per minute. Interfire on C.T. Brune C.T. C.18.c.47 to C.18 c.82.22, fixed 2000. From 12 midnight to 2 a.m 29.7.17 Armentieres heavily bombarded with Shrapnel, H.S. & gas shells. Huge casualties among civilians.	AM
"	29		Enemy still in morning ARMENTIERES heavily shelled with shrapnel – gas shells HE. The fire eased the previous day owing	

Army Form C. 2118.

WAR DIARY
of 173 Machine Gun Coy.
INTELLIGENCE SUMMARY.
(Erase heading not required.)

JULY 1917. Page 4.

Place	Date	Hour	Summary of Events and Information	Remarks and references to Appendices
ARMENTIERES DEFENCES	July 30.		Heavy shelling commenced in ARMENTIERES at 8 a.m. & continued throughout today — gas shells at intervals. — 15 o.r. wounded in action (gas)	1917.
	July 31.		Enemy continued shelling ARMENTIERES through-out heavy. Lt. FLETCHER E.A. & 2nd Lt FISHER W.F. wounded in action. 21 o.r. wounded in action (gas).	KR.

Army Form C. 2118.

WAR DIARY
of 173 Machine Gun Company.
INTELLIGENCE SUMMARY.
(Erase heading not required.)

AUGUST 1917.

Place	Date	Hour	Summary of Events and Information	Remarks and references to Appendices
ARMENTIERES DEFENCES.	Aug 1.		Strength of Company 1 Aug 1917. 10 officers 129 other ranks	173
"	" 2		A quieter day. 3 o.r. wounded (gas) from gas shelling in vicinity	173
"	" 3		All quiet in ARMENTIERES. 3 o.r. wounded (gas) do. 2.Lt. BURNETT reported back from Rest Camp	173
"	" 4		Quiet during the day. At 11 p.m. Enemy commenced heavy bombardment of town with gas shells.	173
"	" 5		Enemy continued shelling till 2 a.m. with gas shells. Reinforcements of 26 o.r. arrived. 152 on strength	173
"	" 6		A quieter day. Shelling at intervals in HOUPLINES & ARMENTIERES. 180 o.r. of 170 Bde attached to this Company for duty took over the infantry defences of ARMENTIERES. Heavy shelling during tonight from 10pm	173
"	" 7		"Quiet" except for shelling in N. HOUPLINES throughout the day. 18 o.r. attached from 170 & Bde to act as guides for work on infantry defences of town. 1 o.r. killed.	173
"			Continued shelling in N. HOUPLINES near the Sluice Lock. 11 o.r. arrived as reinforcements	173
"	" 8		2nd Lt. Sykes taken on strength of Company. Capt NEEDHAM returned to Coy from leave.	173
"	" 9		A quieter day. Enemy aircraft active at night.	173
"	" 10		Quiet in ARMENTIERES during day. 8 o.r. attached from 170 Bd. 13 & 15 Cheshires Shelling 1 ARMENTIERES during day light. Draft of 32 arrived to company. 21 Reinforcements to 172 My Coy.	173
"	" 11		Enemy shelling in early morning + bombs dropped in Town by enemy aircraft.	173
"	" 12		Enemy artillery active on back areas. 2 Enemy aeroplanes engaged by Lewis Guns from anti aircraft mountings - 3000 rounds fired on enemy aircraft during the night.	173

WAR DIARY

of O/C 173 MACHINE GUN COY.

Army Form C. 2118.

INTELLIGENCE SUMMARY. August 1917 Page II

Place	Date	Hour	Summary of Events and Information	Remarks and references to Appendices
ARMENTIERES DEFENCES	1917 Aug 12		Enemy artillery very active – ARMENTIERES shelled continuously throughout the day. HOUPLINES & Bois aven again shelled. 3000 rounds expended by us on indirect fire.	MS
	" 13		Enemy again shelled ARMENTIERES during the day & night. Several fires started during the evening. Battene heavily shelled.	MS
	" 14		A quiet day – considerably less hostile shelling in ARMENTIERES. 3000 rounds expended on indirect fire.	MS
	" 15		Unusually quiet day. Hostile aeroplanes dropped a few bombs on ARMENTIERES during the night. Houplines & back areas shelled intermittently with gas & H.E. 1000 rounds expended by us on indirect fire.	FSF
	" 16		Very little hostile artillery activity in ARMENTIERES. Enemy planes active during morning & night. One was engaged by our M.G. fire. 2500 rds expended in indirect fire	FSF
	" 17		Suggestion by Brigadier that L.G. and aircraft batteries be formed, in addition to the guns used in this war. Quiet day in ARMENTIERES. A few bombs dropped at night by hostile aircraft	FSF
	" 18		Enemy planes active in ARMENTIERES day & night, dropping bombs at irregular intervals. Very little hostile artillery activity. 6000 rounds expended on indirect fire & 1250 on anti-aircraft fire.	FSF
	" 19		Enemy planes less active. O.C. 5C 9.5 shelled with H.E. Shrapnel. 6000 rounds expended on indirect fire	FSF

WAR DIARY
or INTELLIGENCE SUMMARY

of 173 MACHINE GUN COY.

Page III — August 1917

Army Form C. 2118.

Place	Date	Hour	Summary of Events and Information	Remarks and references to Appendices
ARMENTIERES DEFENCES	1917 Aug 20		Our Battery of 4 M.G.s opened Machine gun barrage at H6 & 9O95. Some hostile artillery activity in the town of ARMENTIERES. Some enemy planes appeared, but a few bombs were dropped. 9000 rounds expended on Indirect fire.	
	21		Very quiet day. 5500 rounds expended on Indirect fire.	
	22		Slight hostile artillery activity from 7pm & 9pm around C25d, otherwise a quiet day. Bombs dropped around Transport lines, and "falling" between two civilians.	
	23		Heavy bombardment for about an hour around C25d. at 8am, followed by a quiet day. 1 gas alarm sounded at about midnight 23/24, but no gas was noticed in chief points.	
	24		Nothing of importance. 8500 rounds expended in Indirect Fire.	
	25		Nothing of importance. 7560 rounds expended on Indirect Fire.	
	26		Our Anti-aircraft position at H6 & 9O95 barely shelled. Casualties – 1 O.R. wounded	
	27		Very quiet day. 3000 rounds expended in Indirect fire	
	28		Nothing of importance. 8500 rounds expended in Indirect fire.	
	29		A quiet day – Visibility bad – 8000 rounds in Indirect fire	1077
	30		Slight hostile artillery activity on HOULINES – 9000 rounds in indirect fire.	113
	31		A quiet day – nothing to report. Strength of Company 24/8/17. 11 officers 176 O.R.	111

WAR DIARY of 173 MACHINE GUN COMPANY

INTELLIGENCE SUMMARY. SEPTEMBER 1917. Vol 5 PAGE I.

Place	Date	Hour	Summary of Events and Information	Remarks and references to Appendices
ARMENTIERES DEFENCES	1917 1 Sep	Strength of Company 3 officers 176 o.r.	A quiet day. 8000 rounds expended by us in indirect fire	143
"	2 Sep		Hostile artillery activity increased in HOUPLINES and ARMENTIERES. 7000 rounds expended in indirect fire.	143
"	3 -		Considerable aerial activity - several enemy planes were engaged by our AA machine gun. Hostile artillery	
"			again increased in HOUPLINES Sector. During the day we fired on C 23.d 34.69 (Hostile T.M. position) from	143.
"	4 -		shell the Battalion in the line had received 30 (fifty rounds) 5000 rounds in indirect fire.	
"	5 -		Visibility good - great aerial activity. We again fired on C 23 d 34.69 during the day - 3000 rounds expended	143.
"	6 -		ARMENTIERES and back areas shelled at intervals during the day - 5000 rounds in indirect fire	143
"			The neighbourhood of the billets in ARMENTIERES were shelled heavily during the afternoon - during the	
"			a horse belonging to Company was got on fire and the H.Q. becoming temporarily until the	143.
"	7 -		fire was extinguished - 5000 rounds in indirect fire.	
"	8 -		A quiet day. nothing of importance to report. 5000 rounds in indirect fire	143.
"			Nothing of importance to report. 5000 rounds in indirect fire	143.
"	9 -		A quiet day. A few Casualties in back area were shelled. 4000 rounds in indirect fire	143
"	10 -		Nothing of importance to report. 4000 rounds in indirect fire	143
"	11 -		Enemy shelled back areas without doing much damage. 4000 rounds by us in indirect fire	143
"	12		A quiet day	143
"	13		Nothing of importance to report.	143
"	14		do do	143

WAR DIARY
of 173 Machine Gun Company
INTELLIGENCE SUMMARY. September 1917. Page II.

Army Form C.-2118.

Place	Date	Hour	Summary of Events and Information	Remarks and references to Appendices
Armentieres Defences	1917 Sep 15	-	A quiet day - Nothing to report	M
	16	-	do	M
	17	-	During the morning the Coys relieved by 176 M.G.Coy. 38th Division and proceeded to Rest Billets at Steenwerck	M
	18	-	On rest Billets at Steenwerck.	M
	19	-	The Company marched from Steenwerck into billets at La Gorgue.	M
	20	-	The Company marched from La Gorgue to Lamiquellerie	M
	21	-	The Company marched from La Miquellerie to Training Area and took up billets at La Tirmand	M
	22 to 30	-	Training at La Tirmand under 170th Bde Instructions and administration	IIIB.

WAR DIARY
of
173 MACHINE GUN COMPANY
INTELLIGENCE SUMMARY
OCTOBER 1917

Army Form C. 2118.

(Erase heading not required.)

Instructions regarding War Diaries and Intelligence Summaries are contained in F. S. Regs, Part II. and the Staff Manual respectively. Title pages will be prepared in manuscript.

Place	Date	Hour	Summary of Events and Information	Remarks and references to Appendices
Oct. 1.	1917		Strength of Company 11 officers 176 O.R.	AA3
LA TIRMAND	Oct 1-5		On rest Billets at LA TIRMAND.	AA3
"	-5		2nd LTs BRIANT & SYKES with one section and transport left the Company for duty purposes.	AA3
"	5-16		On rest Billets at LA TIRMAND	AA3
"	17		Proceeded from LA TIRMAND to RENESCURE	AA3
"	18		Moved from RENESCURE to PROVEN	AA3
"	18-23		On rest camp at PROVEN	AA3
"	23		Proceeded from PROVEN to BOESINGHE thence to MARSOUIN CAMP	AA3
"	24		A & D Sections under 2nd LTs CARPENTER & BROCK moved into the Barrage line at 19 metre Hill – Company H.Q. being established at DROP HOUSE	AA3
"	25		A & D Sections withdrew from Barrage line and the Company proceeded to new Barrage line extending from a point 100x due N. of FERDAN HOUSE along a line 320° (T.B.) 200x in length. relieved by B Section	AA3
"	26		At 5.40 p.m. in accordance with instructions from Dvn. G. O. a barrage was fired to cover the advance of 170 Infantry Brigade (see Appendix attached). 2/Lt G.T. Harrison wounded. at 5 p.m. enemy barrage put down over our barrage line. 14 casualties	AA3
"	27		Barrage line held by A, B & D Sections	AA3
"	28		A & D Sections withdrawn. B Section remaining with 6 guns	AA3
"	29.30.31		B Section relieved by A & D Sections under 2nd Lt CARPENTER. 2 O.R. killed. No further change.	AA3

Army Form C. 2118.

WAR DIARY
of 173 MACHINE GUN COMPANY
INTELLIGENCE SUMMARY
NOVEMBER 1917
Vol 7

(Erase heading not required.)

Instructions regarding War Diaries and Intelligence Summaries are contained in F. S. Regs., Part II. and the Staff Manual respectively. Title pages will be prepared in manuscript.

Place	Date	Hour	Summary of Events and Information	Remarks and references to Appendices
LANGEMARCK	1st		Strength of Company 1st Nov. 8 officers 113 o.r.	
	2nd		A&D Section in Barrage line 100x N of FERDAN HOUSE	MB
			B Section under 2Lt NISBET relieved A&D Section	MB
	3rd		Harassing Fire carried out by us on arranged targets	MB
"	4th		do. At 5.30 a.m. a Barrage was fired by us.	MB
"	5.		A&D Section under 2Lt CARPENTER relieved B Section	MB
"	6		At 6.0 a.m. a Company Barrage was fired by us in conjunction with operations in PASSCHENDAELE Sector	MB
"	7		At 4.40 p.m. The Company was relieved by 246 M.G. Coy (17th Div) & proceeded to BOESINGHE	MB
BOESINGHE	8.		At BOESINGHE. Entrained at BOESINGHE Station at 8.30pm	MB
	9.		Proceeded by train from BOESINGHE to AUDRUICQ & from there marched to CLERQUES	MB
CLERQUES	10		In rest Billets at CLERQUES	MB
"	10 to 30		In rest Billets at CLERQUES	MB
			Strength of Company 30/11/17 9 officers 107 o.r.	MB

T2134. Wt. W708—776. 500000. 4/15. Sir J. C. & S.

Army Form C. 2118.

WAR DIARY OF 173 MACHINE GUN COMPANY
INTELLIGENCE SUMMARY.

(Erase heading not required.)

DECEMBER 1917

Instructions regarding War Diaries and Intelligence Summaries are contained in F. S. Regs., Part II. and the Staff Manual respectively. Title pages will be prepared in manuscript.

Vol 8

Place	Date Dec 17	Hour	Summary of Events and Information	Remarks and references to Appendices
CLERQUES	1		Strength of Company 9 officers 105 o.r.	A19
"	1–7		In rest. Billets at CLERQUES	A19
HERZEELE	7		The Company entrained from AUDRUICQ to PROVEN marching from there to billets at HERZEELE	A19
"	7–16		In billets at HERZEELE	A19
"	16		2nd Lt CARPENTER with 4 guns of A Section proceeded to the line and took up position at SIGNAL FARM	A19
"	17		The Company entrained for PROVEN marching from there to SUTTON CAMP. Capt. N.S. Sturgy.	
SUTTON CAMP			MANSERGH attached to the Company as 2nd i/c vice CAPT. E. NEEDHAM.	A19
"	–19		Four guns at SIGNAL FARM removed to MONTMIRAIL FARM (2 guns) and JAPAN HOUSE (2 guns)	A19
"	–20		Reinforcement of 18 o.r. from Base + 6 o.r. from 173 In.g. Coy received	A19
"	–21		Reinforcement of 21 o.r. transferred from No 3 M.G.Coy.	A19
"	–24		Four guns of A Section relieved by 4 teams of B Section under 2nd LT NISBET. 4 guns of B Section under 2nd LT PENELLY and 4 guns of D Section under 2nd LT BROOK took up positions on the line. Forward Coy. HQ removed to SIGNAL FARM.	A19
LUNEVILLE FARM	26		Remainder of Coy moved from SUTTON CAMP to LUNEVILLE FARM (DUEZINGHE Line)	A19
DUBLIN CAMP	28.		Remainder of Coy moved from LUNEVILLE FARM to DUBLIN CAMP. 1 o.r. wounded by bomb.	A19
"	29		A complete Section with transport gun etc. under Lt GARDNER A.A. + 2nd LT EMERSON R.S. arrived ex Cadre of Company 11 Officers 197 o.r.	
			Its strength of the Company on Section forward overseas in October. Strength of Company 11 Officers 197 o.r.	A19

Army Form C. 2118.

WAR DIARY OF 173 MACHINE GUN COMPANY

INTELLIGENCE SUMMARY

(Erase heading not required.)

JANUARY 1918 PAGE 1

Instructions regarding War Diaries and Intelligence Summaries are contained in F.S. Regs., Part II. and the Staff Manual respectively. Title pages will be prepared in manuscript.

Place	Date	Hour	Summary of Events and Information	Remarks and references to Appendices
DUBLIN CAMP.	1		Strength of Company 10 officers 197 O.R.	
"	1		12 guns of the Company relieved by 8 guns of 53 Machine Gun Company - Coy HQ at DUBLIN CAMP	173
"	3		Transport section of Company march to STEENWERCK AREA.	173
"	4		Company entrained at INTERNATIONAL CORNER for BAILLEUL marching from there to Billets in ARMENTIERES - C DPT	173
			C.HQ SHEPHERD FORK on arrival of the Company from CAPT N.S.J.G. MANSERGH	
ARMENTIERES	5		A, B & D Section relieved 12 guns of 23rd A.M.F.Coy in battery positions at HOUPLINES, 4 guns of B Section took over	
DEFENCES			Anti-aircraft position in ARMENTIERES Company HQ at RUE SAM CARNOT No.18. ARMENTIERES.	173	O.O. No.1 att.d
			Section HQ D Section. BREWERY HOUPLINES. A.113 Section TISSAGE HOUPLINES.		
"	6		A quiet day with occasional shelling in ARMENTIERES	173
"	7		Nothing to report	173
"	8		Nothing to report.	173
"	10		Considerable hostile shelling of hostile position in ARMENTIERES	173
"	11		The following S.O.S. emplacements were manned by one-man teams of the Company D Section FARM PIT		O.O. No.2 att.d
			HERRING CORNER, DURHAM CASTLE, JAMES CORNER with Sect HQ at THE BREWERY. HOUPLINES		
			B. Section, EISPERS HOPE, KENNETH PLACE, LES RETREAT JALLANS POINT with Section		
			HQ at TISSAGE: A Section, HELENE, SIBERIA, FOLKESTONE, BOULOGNE with Section		
			HQ at C27.c.4590. C SECTION, LA MAISON MUND, LEICESTER YEO OMARES NEST with		
			Section HQ at 7.1.c.5.9. The barrage position taken over were abandoned		

Army Form C. 2118.

WAR DIARY
of 173 MACHINE GUN COMPANY
INTELLIGENCE SUMMARY

(Erase heading not required.)

JANUARY 1918   PAGE 2.

Instructions regarding War Diaries and Intelligence Summaries are contained in F. S. Regs., Part II. and the Staff Manual respectively. Title pages will be prepared in manuscript.

Place	Date	Hour	Summary of Events and Information	Remarks and references to Appendices
ARMENTIERES DEFENCES	1918			
	Jan 12		Battery positions in ARMENTIERES were shelled during the afternoon.	177
"	" 13		A quiet day with nothing to report.	173
"	" 14			
"	" 15		Nothing to report.	173
"	" 16			
"	" 17		Indirect fire carried out by us on enemy's talk company HP. strench. 24,000 rounds expended	177
"	" 18		A quiet day in ARMENTIERES. Indirect fire carried out by us on various targets behind enemy's lines, 13000 rounds expended.	
	19		Various Battery Positions in ARMENTIERES shelled throughout the day	
	20		Large increase in hostile artillery activity. Indirect fire programme carried out, against various targets behind enemy lines. Ordered to cease fire at 8/10 15000 rounds expended.	
	21		ARMENTIERES shelled intermittently throughout the day.	
	22		Usual hostile artillery fire in ARMENTIERES.	
	23		Exceptionally quiet day in ARMENTIERES, no shells falling in the town. 5 guns mounted on S.O.S. Barrage line in N. HOUPLINES	

WAR DIARY
of 173 MACHINE GUN COMPANY
INTELLIGENCE SUMMARY

JANUARY 1918 — Page 2

Army Form C. 2118.

Place	Date	Hour	Summary of Events and Information	Remarks and references to Appendices
ARMENTIÈRES DEFENCES	1918			
	Jan 24		Slight increase in hostile artillery fire in ARMENTIÈRES.	J.S.P.
	25		Considerable shell activity in & around ARMENTIÈRES. A quiet day.	J.S.P.
	26		Extremely quiet day. Low visibility resulted in little aerial and artillery activity in ARMENTIÈRES.	A.W.B. M.W.E
	27			M.W.E
	28		Another very quiet day. Owing to mist Observation was poor. The following redistribution of M.G's took place:- B Section under 2/Lt Brock were relieved at FARM POST, JAMES CORNER, DURHAM CASTLE, and HERRING CORNER by a Section from 175th M.G. Coy under 2/Lt BROSTER. This Section became attached to 173? M.G. Coy for rations and discipline. D Section 173? Inf. Coy on being relieved took up a Reserve Position at I.14.c. 60.80. in the vicinity of the RUE FLEURIE SWITCH, and come under the order of the G.O.C. 170th Inf. Bde.	CO. No 3 A.W.B. CAP.S
	29		From 7am to 12 noon the enemy shelled near H.12 central with 5.9 H.E. This was repeated for a short time about 4.p.m. There was an increase in Aerial activity and enemy M.G's fired intermittently during the night.	CAP.S
	30		Enemy artillery rather more active in the back areas. Shells falling N. of the HOUPLINES-ARMENTIÈRES road.	AW.B.

Army Form C. 2118.

Instructions regarding War Diaries and Intelligence Summaries are contained in F.S. Regs., Part II. and the Staff Manual respectively. Title pages will be prepared in manuscript.

WAR DIARY
or
INTELLIGENCE SUMMARY.
(Erase heading not required.)

Place	Date	Hour	Summary of Events and Information	Remarks and references to Appendices
ARMENTIERES DEFENCES.	Jan. 30		During the night a dummy raid was carried out by the Infantry. A and D Sections cooperated with Indirect fire, 10,000 rounds being expended on the following targets – T.5.b.20.30 and T.16.b.90.30 & T.17a.70.15.	CWR&L
	31		The day was quiet with a minute which increased towards evening. In accordance with arrangements made for a raid by 2/9th K.L.R. C & D Sections took up positions at C.4.a.92.57 and T.14.d.10.90 respectively, in order to put up a Box Barrage. The raid however was cancelled and the guns resumed their normal positions.	CWR&L

T2134. Wt. W708—776. 500000. 4/15. Sir J.C. & S.

SECRET.   173. MACHINE GUN COMPANY.   COPY NO.: 7
                 Operation Order No. 1.

1. The 173. M. G. Coy. will relieve the 23rd. Australian
   M. G. Coy. on the 5th. inst, as follows:--

(a) Section 2Lt. Carpenter, will relieve one section = 4 guns
    at TISSAGE.

(b) Section 2Lt. Nisbet, will relieve one Section = 4 guns
    at TISSAGE.

(c) Section Lt. Gardner and 2Lt. Emerson, will relieve one
    section = 4 guns employed on Anti Aircraft work in ARMENTIERES

(D) SECTION 2LT. Brock & 2Lt. Houghton will relieve one Section =
    4 guns at the BREWERY.

2. Sections will meet their guides at Coy H. Q. at 9 a.m.
   on the 5th. instant.

3. Tripods and ten Belt Boxes per gun will be taken over.
   O's C. Sections must state on their receipts that these
   were taken over in a clean and satisfactory condition.

4. All Trench Stores will be taken over and a copy of receipt
   sent to Coy. H. Q.

5. Sections will parade in Marching order and will carry the
   unexpended portion of the days rations with them.

6. The Transport Officer will arrange for transport to take
   guns, spare parts, blankets etc to Section H. Q.

7. Rations will be sent up for the 6th; inst, under arrange-
   ments which will be notified later.

8. Relief complete will be reported in writing to Coy.
   H. Q. by 3-0 p.m.

9. ACKNOWLEDGE.

   Issued at 7. p.m. 4/1/18.

   Copies to:-

   1, 2; 3;& 4 O's C. Sections.
   5. D.M.G.O.
   6. Transport Officer.
   7. & 8. War Diary.
   9. File.

                                        C H Shepherd
                                        Capt.
                                    O. C. 173. Machine Gun Coy

SECRET.   173. Machine Gun Company.
               Operation Orders No. 2.   Copy No. 8.

1. In compliance with 171st. Inf. Bde. B.M. 1268 the 16
   guns of this company will be disposed as follows :--

   D. Section   FARM POST,   HERRING CORNER
                 Durham Castle   JAMES CORNER

   B. Section   FISHERS HOLE   LEO'S RETREAT
                 ALLANS POSSE   KENNETHS PRIDE

   A. Section   FOLKESTONE   BOULOGNE
                 HELENE   SIBERIA

   C. Section   LEICESTER YEO, MOUND, LA MAISON,
                 MARES NEST.

2. Section H.Q. will be as follows :-
      A. Section.   C 26 b 90.00
      B. Section.   C 27 b 50.70
      C. Section.   I 2 60.60
      D. Section.   C 21 b 50.20

3. Each Section will maintain a garrison of 2 men per gun
   actually at the gun position. The remainder will be at
   Section H.Q.

4. An Observation Post will be selected by each Section Officer
   and kept manned day and night by two men who will be
   responsible for alarming the gun teams in the case of an
   attack or gas.

5. The disposition of guns as laid down in para.1. will take
   effect from 12 noon 11.1.18. O.C.'s Sections will report
   occupation complete as soon as possible after 12 nooN 11.1.18.

6. ACKNOWLEDGE.
              Issued at 6 P;M; 10.1.18.
   Copies to -   1. G.O.C. 171st. Inf. Bde.
                  2,3,4,5. O's C. Sections.
                  6 D.M.G.O.
                  7. 171st. M.G. Coy.
                  8 & 9 War Diary.
                  10. File.

                              (S
                                                    Capt.,
                         173 Machine Gun Company.,

SECRET.   COPY NO. 2

173. MACHINE GUN COMPANY.
OPERATION ORDER NO. 3.

1. "D" section, 173. M. G. Coy. (4 guns) will be relieved by No. 4. section, 171st. M. G. Coy. (4 guns) at worth Houplines in the following emplacements. FARM POST, HERRING CORNER, DURHAM CASTLE, JAMES CORNER, on the 28th inst

2. One guide for section W. O. will be at TISSAGE at 10 a.m. Four guides (1 per gun) will be at TISSAGE at 11 a.m.

3. All Trench stores standing orders S.A.A. range cards etc, will be handed over.

4. Relief complete will be wired using word "FINI"

5. On completion of relief " D " section, 173.M. G. Coy will occupy positions in SPRING FARM.

6. Two signallers of 173 M. G. Coy. will report to O. C. " D " section by 10 a. m. and will relieve the two signallers already there who will move with " D " section to SPRING FARM with 1 D 3 telephone.

7. D sections fighting Limbers will be at the BREWERY at 12 noon

8. O. C. " D " section will report when he has occupied SPRING FARM. This report must be sent in BY 5 p.m.

9. ACKNOWLEDGE.

Issued at 5 p.m.
27. 1. 18.

Signed C.H.P. Shepherd
CAPTAIN.
O. C. 173. M. GUN COY.

Copies to:--
1 to O.C. " D " section
2 & 3 WAR DIARY.
4. FILE.

WAR DIARY of 173 MACHINE GUN COMPANY

INTELLIGENCE SUMMARY for FEBRUARY 1918 Page (1)

Army Form C. 2118.

Place	Date	Hour	Summary of Events and Information	Remarks and references to Appendices
ARMENTIERES DEFENCES	FEB 1		The day was quiet up till 8.30.p.m. when a raid was carried out by the 2/9th K.L.R. The guns of C and D Sections took part in the protective barrage put up by M.G's and the Artillery. Positions and Tasks as follows:- C Section. Battery position (4 guns under 2/Lt GARDNER) C 4 a 92.56. Task-Northern Leg of Box Barrage from I 11 c 50.70 to I 17 a 95.65. D Section. Battery position (4 guns under 2/Lt BROCK) I 14 d 10.90. Task-Southern Leg of Box Barrage from I 16 d 95.30 to I 17 a 40.65. Fire was opened at Zero (8.30 p.m.) and continued until 9.20.p.m., each Battery expending 14,000 rounds - a Total of 28,000. The raid was a complete success, three prisoners being taken, and considerable damage done to the enemy trenches. Our casualties were nil. The enemy's retaliation was feeble.	Ref Map. Part of Sheet 36 NW HOUPLINES 1:10,000 36 NW.4. BOIS GRENIER 1:10,000 C/H/S/
	2		The weather became fine and bright, and in consequence there was an increase in aerial activity on both sides. Our own artillery, and also that of the enemy, was quiet.	C/H/S/

WAR DIARY of 173 MACHINE GUN COMPANY

INTELLIGENCE SUMMARY for February 1918

Army Form C. 2118.

Page 2

Place	Date	Hour	Summary of Events and Information	Remarks and references to Appendices
ARMENTIERES DEFENCES	FEB 3		A quiet day. Our artillery were active between 4 and 5 a.m. The enemy's activity was normal. In accordance with orders received from the D.M.G.O. The guns of "C" Section (MARES NEST, LA MAISON, MOUND and LEICESTER YEO) were employed in pairs on A.A. Work, emplacements being constructed at T.1.d.12.59 and T.1.d.76.74 (Sheet 36 N.W.4 BOIS-GRENIER 1:10,000).	Attd
	4		A fine day with considerable aerial activity. The enemy's artillery was more active the neighbourhood of BUTERNE LANE, C.27.C.40.65, being shelled between 1 & 2 p.m. The FRY PAN – LA VESÉE area was shelled with "5.9" between 2 and 3 a.m.	Attd
	5		On a new Divisional Defence Scheme coming into force a redistribution of M.g's took place. A Section (2/Lt CARPENTER) were relieved at HÉLÈNE, SIBERIA, FOLKESTONE, and BOULOGNE by a section from the 172nd M.G. Coy. This relief was completed at 12.30 p.m. A Section passed into the Divisional Reserve under the D.M.G.O. and proceeded to billets at ERQUINGHEM LAUNDRY. There was considerable increase the activity of the enemy's artillery. About 500 shells mostly "5.9" fell into ARMENTIERES, near the cross roads, RUE SADI CARNOT	

WAR DIARY
or
INTELLIGENCE SUMMARY.

Army Form C. 2118.

(3)

Place	Date	Hour	Summary of Events and Information	Remarks and references to Appendices
ARMENTIÈRES DEFENCES	FEB 5		RUE NATIONALE C.25.c.30.30 (Sheet 36.N.W.2.N.E.1. 1:10,000), during the day. The BANDSTAND and Batteries near were also shelled during the morning. The enemy aircraft were active, 3 bombs being dropped near C Section's H.Q. I.1.d 52.70 (Sheet 36.N.W.4. 1:10,000)	etttt
	6		The day was fairly quiet with the exception of hostile retaliation for our covering barrage in support of the raid carried out by the 2/7 K.L.R. This took place at 8.30.p.m. 5 M.Gs of the Company cooperated under 57th Div Barrage Group subsisting from 8.30.p.m. until 9 p.m. Positions and Targets :- One gun (B Section) under 2/Lt NISBET fired from C 27 c 55·85 at C 23 c 86·75, and 4 guns (C Section) under Lt GARDNER fired from I 3 c 80·10 at I 29 c 37·05 to I 29 d 70·70. Total number of rounds fired 16,750. The raid was successful, 10 prisoners and a light M.G. being captured.	etttt
	7		A quiet day. During the morning a few whizz-bangs fell in the vicinity of TISSAGE. Lt Col HOPE. D.S.O. (O.C. M.G. Battalion.) visited Coy H.Q.	etttt
	8		Quiet day with nothing to report.	etttt

Army Form C. 2118.

WAR DIARY
or
INTELLIGENCE SUMMARY.
(Erase heading not required.)

Instructions regarding War Diaries and Intelligence Summaries are contained in F.S. Regs., Part II. and the Staff Manual respectively. Title pages will be prepared in manuscript.

(4)

Place	Date	Hour	Summary of Events and Information	Remarks and references to Appendices
ARMENTIERES DEFENCES	FEB 9		A few hostile shells reported to have fallen near C 27 b 7.3 during the afternoon. Otherwise very little activity.	
	10		Our artillery was quiet during the day, but a heavy bombardment took place on the front of the Sector North of the LYS between 10 & 11 p.m. Owing to a high wind there was very little aerial activity.	CHSS
	11		A quiet day. An A.A. position was constructed at I 2 c 40.75 and a Lewis gun mounted there.	CHSS CHSS
	12		Very quiet - nothing to report	
	13		Quiet. Preparations to handing over made. The line of fire of KENNETH'S PRIDE was altered to a grid bearing of 30°	CHSS Ref. O.O. 4 attd.
	14		The Company were relieved by 176th M.G. Coy (38th Division). On relief the Company was billeted for the night in ARMENTIERES. 2/Lt R.P.V. CARPENTER and Billeting Party proceeded by lorry to Billeting area near ESTAIRES	@ IHSS
ARMENTIERES	15		The Company paraded at 9 a.m. to march to Billets which were reached at 12.30 p.m. The route was through ERQUINGHEM, BAC-ST-MAUR, ESTAIRES to CHAPELLE	

Army Form C. 2118.

WAR DIARY
or
INTELLIGENCE SUMMARY.
(Erase heading not required.)

(5)

Place	Date	Hour	Summary of Events and Information	Remarks and references to Appendices
CHAPELLE DUVELLE (ESTAIRES)	FEB 15		DUVELLE, Coy H.Q. being situated at L26 b.00.20	CAH8L
"	16		The day was spent in cleaning and overhauling clothing, guns and equipment. A conference of O.C. Coys was held at Bn. H.Q.	CAH8L
"	17		Kit inspection held during the morning.	CAH8L
"	18	7.45 a.m	Inspection. 9-10 a.m. Squad Drill with Arms 10-11 a.m. Elementary Gun Drill 11.15 am – 12 noon Stripping 12-1 pm Musketry T.S.O's parade 1-1.15 pm Ceremonial	CAH8L
"	19	5.30 pm lecture to Officers & N.C.O's of the Bn H.Q. by Lect Hope D.S.O. 7.45 am Inspection 9-10 am Mechanism 10-11 am Drill with Arms & Signal Drill. 11.15 am - 12 noon Immediate Action 12-1 pm Musketry T.S.O's parade 1-1.15 pm Ceremonial		CAH8L
"	20	7.45 am	Inspection. 9-10 am Squad Drill & Arms Drill 10-11 am Elementary Gun Drill 11.15 a.m - 12 noon map reading & Scouting 12-1 pm Musketry T.S.O's parade. 1-1.15 pm Ceremonial.	CAH8L
"	21	7.45 a.m	Inspection. 9-10 am Musketry & Squad Drill 10-11 am T.O.E.T. 11.15 a.m - 12 noon Combined Drill 12-1 pm Musketry T.S.O's parade . 1-1.15 pm Ceremonial	CAH8L
"	22	7.45 a.m	Inspection. 9-10 am Squad Drill & Arms Drill 10-11 a.m. T.O.E.T. 11.15 a.m - 12 noon map reading & bombwork. 12-1 pm Musketry T.S.O's parade . 1-1.15 pm Ceremonial	CAH8L

T2134. Wt. W708—776. 500000. 4/15. Sir J.C. & S.

Army Form C. 2118.

WAR DIARY
or
INTELLIGENCE SUMMARY.
(Erase heading not required.)

Instructions regarding War Diaries and Intelligence Summaries are contained in F. S. Regs., Part II. and the Staff Manual respectively. Title pages will be prepared in manuscript.

(6)

Place	Date	Hour	Summary of Events and Information	Remarks and references to Appendices
CHAPELLE DUVELLE (ESTAIRES)	FEB 23	7.45 a.m.	Inspection. 9-10 a.m. Squad Drill & Arms Drill. 10-11 a.m. T.O.E.T. 11.15 a.m.–12 noon. I.A. 12–1 pm Musketry. F.S.O's Parade. 1–1.15 pm Ceremonial.	C.H.R.L
	24	9.30 a.m.	Inspection. 10 a.m. Kit Inspection. 11 a.m.–12 noon. Mechanism and Stripping for Backward men. Services. R.C. MERVILLE. 9 a.m. C.E. (Voluntary) 3 pm. 13 Wells	C.H.R.L
	25	7.45 a.m.	Inspection. 9-10 a.m. P.T and Squad Drill. 10-11 a.m. T.O.E.T. 11.15-11.45 a.m. Musketry. 11.45–12.45 pm Barrage Drill. 12.45–1.15 pm Map & Compass. 5.30 pm Lecture to Officers and N.C.O's by Major. Grierson D.S.O.	C.H.R.L
	26	7.45 a.m.	Inspection. 9-10 a.m. P.T and Arms Drill. 10-11 a.m. Action from Pack Animals. 11.15-11.45 a.m. Musketry. 11.45–12.45 pm Elevating & Traversing Dials, Clinometer & Level. 12.45–1.15 pm. I.A.	C.H.R.L
	27	7.45 a.m.	Inspection. 9-10 a.m. P.T and Ceremonial. 10-11 a.m. Barrage Drill. 11.15–11.45 a.m. Musketry. 11.45 a.m.–12.45 a.m. Belt-filling. 12.45–1.15 pm Care and Cleaning	C.H.R.L
	28		During the morning Baths and Inspection by M.O. In the afternoon C & D Sections carried out Musketry Practice on Range	

SECRET.   173rd. M. G. Coy.
           OPERATION ORDER NO. 4.   COPY No: ...6..

1. The 173rd. M. G. Coy. will be relieved by the 176th. M. G. Coy. on the 14th. instant.

2. The Coy. after relief will spend the night 14/15 in billets in ARMENTIERES, and on the 15th. will march to their billeting area.

3. Times of reliefs will be notified later.

4. 2Lt. Carpenter. will be incharge of the advance party which will proceed on the 14th. by lorry. This lorry will convey all the heavy baggage of the Coy. including blankets.

5. Billets and all shelters and emplacements will be handed over in a clean condition, and a certificate stating this obtained.

6. On relief sections will proceed to Coy. H. Q. for instruction as to billets.

7. ACKNOWLEDGE.

Issued at 7.P.M. 12/2/18.

Copies to:-

1. 2. 3. 4. O's C. Sections.
5. Transport Sergeant.
6 & 7. War Diary.
8. File.

C H B Shepheard
Capt.
O. C. 173. M. G. Coy.

57. Div A.

Herewith copy my
War Diary for month of
March 1918.

J. M. Tobin
Capt
Comdg 57 Bn M.G.C.

57 Bn M.G Corps

Army Form C. 2118.

WAR DIARY
or
INTELLIGENCE SUMMARY.
(Erase heading not required.)

Instructions regarding War Diaries and Intelligence Summaries are contained in F.S. Regs., Part II. and the Staff Manual respectively. Title pages will be prepared in manuscript.

Place	Date	Hour	Summary of Events and Information	Remarks and references to Appendices
Sheet 36 N.E.			The 57 Batt. M.G.C was formed during the latter part of February and was definitely constituted as a battalion on the 1st March 1918.	
			The Battalion was formed from the personnel of the 170, 171, 173 and 73 M.G Coys.	
			It consisted of 3 Coys: A, B, C, D. Lieut. Col. H. H. Ballard (K.R. Royal T) (4th N.Zeal Manual Reg) from 172 Coy was the C.O. "A" J.M. Shepherd — 173 Coy. Officer wdg H.H. Ballard (K.R Royal T) Res. Co. — 173 Coy.	See Appendix A.
			The reduced scale of formation (MinnKet 44) the battalion was not so far quite treated as follows:	
			H.Q. 1/52 & 7.9 A Coy L/29 6 & 84 B Coy L/29 & 8.5 C Coy L/29 & 120.5	
CHAPELLE DUVELLE	16/7/18		D Coy L/26 & 0.1. The Coys were attached to 172 Inft Brigade for duty in care quite	
	15/3/18		moving through the Polygone Wood. A.C. Coys to be on the duty to collect with being	
			relieved by B,D Coys on March 9th	
	9.3.18	10.30 am	At 10 am the Brenests — on March 9 the Battalion was inspected by the XI Corps	
			Commander Sir M. Ducane K.C.B and the 57th Bn. Commander Major General	
			R.W.R Barnes C.B D.S.O. — Bgr. General Howard as the Brigadier to	
			battalion briefly with the Colonel R. Hankin and the latter about (?) to inspect is.	

Army Form C. 2118.

WAR DIARY
or
INTELLIGENCE SUMMARY.
(Erase heading not required.)

Instructions regarding War Diaries and Intelligence
Summaries are contained in F. S. Regs. Part II.
and the Staff Manual respectively. Title pages
will be prepared in manuscript.

Place	Date	Hour	Summary of Events and Information	Remarks and references to Appendices
[illegible]	21.3.18	10 am	The Machine Gun Batt. to be visible in the division and all things must be to the Commander's attention under the line that he had to manoeuvre the battalion separate to attention the movement of the transport. Major General Ramsay expressed his admiration of the movement of the transport and how the act that became an own attending one as long to her troopship. After first battalion to proceed to France. After the first day had 10 & but were forth of anywhere in the Patrique. Shots were fired the next day. Had 10 & but were forth of anywhere in the Patrique. "V" men been seen to shoot to – nothing between in the shots been moved. Front and troops time to the division afternoon.	
BOIS GRENIER HEVRRAIN			On Road – 11th – 21st, the battalion relieved the 1/12 R.Batt. in the trenches in the FLEURBAIX BOIS GRENIER Sector. R.Hq Ruyts below – C. Coy white Halls – D Coy Waller. Bn A Coy in Reserve at SAILLY. HQ was here located as follows.	
RADINGHEM AUBERS	11.10pm			
			R.A.H.Q. G12b 05. A Coy B16d 01 B Hq H26a 2.0 – C Coy H26d 4.7. D Coy H17a 47. Trench lines G 36.6.5. All the Knights Posts here together except the halting numbers of A.Coy. Three every letter is left no trenching in case of necessity for the defence A hold to be home front in Coy 59 B'warwick front.	[illegible signatures/notes]
CROIX-DU-BAC				

A5834 Wt. W4973 M687 750,000 8/16 D. D. & L. Ltd. Forms/C.2118/13.

WAR DIARY
or
INTELLIGENCE SUMMARY.

(Erase heading not required.)

Army Form C. 2118.

Place	Date	Hour	Summary of Events and Information	Remarks and references to Appendices
CROIX-DU-BAC			Except for the first two days the Enemy the line has been quiet the Battalion suffering only 18 Casualties. As still fire, one remaining at duty, and 14 gas. Some of them seriously. A certain amount of harassing fire was carried out and Assistance given to the infantry in one raid on March 25th Intermats of the line two Coys held in Areas between the Frontier & Support Reserve Lines and suitable for the line: - All arrangements were made for the support of a 2 Coy Raid of the 2/6 K.L.R. (R.B.) but the operation was cancelled by Corps on 30th inst.	See Appendix B.
	31/3/18		C & D Coys were relieved in the line by B & D Coys 40th Bn. M.G.C & marched to ESTAIRES & NOUVEAU MONDE respectively. Counter. I.O.R. killed at Appendix B.	
			A. Coy remained in Reserve at SAILLY.	
			B. Coy remained in the line until relief of 1/2nd April.	
			Bn. HQrs remained at CROIX DU BAC.	

31/3/18

Army Form C. 2118.

Appendix. "A"

WAR DIARY
or
INTELLIGENCE SUMMARY.

Officers with O.

(Erase heading not required.)

Place	Date	Hour	Summary of Events and Information	Remarks and references to Appendices
L'HARELLE DUVELLE	1/3/18		On formation of Bn.	

Lt.Col. J.F.R. Hope. M.S.O. K.R.R.C. Comdg. joined 5.2.18

Major W.A. Grierson. D.S.O. L.N.L.Regt. (T) 2nd in Command 24.2.18

Capt. M.S. St.G. Mansergh. R.Warwick Regt. S.R. (Seconded 17.2.19 A.G.C.) Adjutant 14.2.18.

A/Capt. H.H. Ball 2/9 K.L.R. (T) Qr.Mr. 13.2.18.

Lieut. J.M. Shepherd. M.G.C. T.O. 11.2.18

Lieut. W. Monks. 4/9 K.L.R. (T) attached Bn for duty as Officer. 13.3.18

C.S.M. J.H. Dukes. 2/5 S.L.R. (T) as R.S.M. 22.2.18

R.Q.M.S. S. Martlew. 2/9 K.L.R. (T) R.Q.M.S. 22.2.18

A. Coy.   B. Coy.   C. Coy.   D. Coy.
O.C.Coy A.Maj J.A. Battaclough. M.C.   O.C.Coy A.Maj R.A.T. Miller   O.C.Coy A.Maj G.A. Wade, M.C.   O.C.Coy A.Maj. C.H.B. Shepherd
2/i.c. A/Capt. T.B. Barron.   2/i.c. Capt. V.H. Wells   2/i.c. A.Capt. O. Greenwood.   2/i.c. A.Capt. H. Bushell
Lt. J.S.P. Hall-Patch   Lt. P.W. Dexter   Lt. L.F.M. Ackroyd.   Lt. A.A. Gardner
" D.C. Davis. M.C.   2/Lt. A.D.G. Brown.   " M.G. Vyvyan   " G.V. Brock
" M. Dixon   " F.L. Taylor   " G.H. Gadd   2/Lt R.P.V. Carpenter
" O.W. Davies   " J.O. Broster   " E.C. Jones,   " E. Nisbet
" H.J.D. Day   (joined 3/3/18)   " L.C.H. Chase (joined 27/8)   2/Lt A.D. Erskine (joined 23/5/8)   " L.D. Pengelly
" P.E. Carr   " H.L. Henry   " H.A. Oakeshott   " F.J. Emerson
2/Lt A.S. Soole   " G.C. Tothill   " E.W. Barber   " F. Houghton
" F. Bell   " G.D. Green.   " G.J. Athron
" G.A. Woodward   " F.L. Hedgcock. (wounded)

C.S.M. T. Godwin M.M.   C.S.M. T.W. Meigh   C.S.M. F.E. Emmott. D.C.M.   A/C.S.M. P. Reed

31/3/18.

Army Form C. 2118.

Appendix B.

WAR DIARY
or
INTELLIGENCE SUMMARY.
(Erase heading not required.)

Instructions regarding War Diaries and Intelligence Summaries are contained in F.S. Regs., Part II. and the Staff Manual respectively. Title pages will be prepared in manuscript.

Place	Date	Hour	Summary of Events and Information	Remarks and references to Appendices
Chapelle Duvelle	1-3-18		**Strength on Formation of Battalion.**	
			Officers O.R.	
			43 780	
			Drafts Reinforcements from Base 6.3.18 O.R. 42 30/3/18 O.R. 22	
			Transfer Transferred from Other Units 2/3/18 22 " " 81 O.R.	
			Decrease Transferred to 34 Bn MGC 29-3-18 22	
			Casualties 1-3-18 to 31-3-18	
			Wounded (Shellfire) O.R. 4	Wounded (Gas) O.R. 14	Killed (Shellfire) O.R. 1
			4 - (Assault)		
			140247 Pte Eaton, G. 27/3 89412 L/C Daley, J.A. 23/3 89055 Pte Hodson, A. 31/3/18	
			110618 " Bill, M. 86903 L/C Tydd, P. Place of Burial
			92343 " Rollings, A. 20/3 22011 Pte Smith, T. Map Ref (Sheet 51b N.W.)
			67245 " Crawford, J. 62899 " Pickles, N. 29/3 H.35.c.2.5
				35926 " Mitchellson A.S. 29/3	
				15432 " Downing, A.	
				3912 " Camp, E.	
				3707 " Phillips, E.	
				14613 " Snelling, C. 24/3	
				12779 " Brunskill, H. 24/3	
				11906 " Currey, A.	
				11846 " Morris, W.	
				7017 " Larkin, T.	
				110526 " McCulloch, W. 24/3	
			Transport		Vehicles:	
			Horses Horses+Mules	4 wheeled 2 wheeled	
			Riding H.D. L.D.	54 9	
			29 4 187		
			Strength on last day of Month	Transport	Vehicles:	
			Officers O.R.	Riding H.D. L.D.	4 wheeled 2 wheeled	
			48 891	32 3 191	59 6	31/3/18

A5834 Wt. W4973 M687 750,000 8/16 D. D. & L. Ltd. Forms/C.2118/13.

www.ingramcontent.com/pod-product-compliance
Lightning Source LLC
Chambersburg PA
CBHW081457160426
43193CB00013B/2513